WORKBOOK

Summary, Lessons & Action Prompts

FOR

The Great Disappearance: 31 Ways to be Rapture Ready

A Guide to Dr. David Jeremiah's Book With Action Prompts

Ryan Reads

Copyright © 2023 Ryan Reads

All rights reserved. No part of this publication may be reproduced, copied, or distributed without the express written permission of the publisher. The information contained herein is not to be stored electronically, transferred, or preserved in any database without prior authorization from the publisher or author. Unauthorized use, reproduction, or distribution may lead to legal consequences.

The content presented in this document is designed to provide general insights into the covered topics. It should not be regarded as professional or legal advice. For specialized guidance, it is recommended to engage the services of a qualified professional.

Disclaimer

Kindly be aware that this publication is not authored by **Dr. David Jeremiah** and holds no affiliation with them. Crafted independently by **Ryan Reads**, this is an enlightening overview and workbook that offers meticulous insights and in-depth analysis of the original book.

Our intention is to furnish readers with valuable insights and inspire exploration of the primary work. However, it is important to note that this publication does not substitute the original piece. We earnestly advise readers to acquire the original work for a comprehensive grasp of the subject matter.

Free Gift

🎁 Your Exclusive Bonus Offer 🎁

As a heartfelt thank you for choosing our workbook, we're excited to present you with an exclusive gift: **five of our incredible workbooks COMPLETELY FREE OF CHARGE.**

Unlock all these complimentary resources by **scanning the QR code provided below**.

But wait, there's more! We're also including the **AUDIOBOOK VERSION** of this very workbook, allowing you to immerse yourself in its content wherever you go. You can access the **FREE AUDIOBOOK** at the end section of this book.

Enjoy your journey with us!

Table of Contents

Disclaimer 3
Free Gift 4
Table of Contents 5
How To Use This Book? 1
Overview Of The Book 4
Chapter 1: Embracing the Imminence 8
    Chapter Summary: 8
        Key Lessons: 8
        Action Prompts (Reflective Questions): 9
        Life Changing Exercises: 14
Chapter 2: Understanding the Signs 15
    Chapter Summary: 15
        Key Lessons: 15
        Action Prompts (Reflective Questions): 17
        Life Changing Exercises: 22
Chapter 3: The Joy of Expectation 23
    Chapter Summary: 23
        Key Lessons: 23
        Action Prompts (Reflective Questions): 25
        Life Changing Exercises: 30
Chapter 4: Strengthening Faith Amidst Chaos 32

Chapter Summary: 32
    Key Lessons: 32
    Action Prompts (Reflective Questions): 33
    Life Changing Exercises: 38

Chapter 5: Facing Fears and Doubts 39

Chapter Summary: 39
    Key Lessons: 39
    Action Prompts (Reflective Questions): 41
    Life Changing Exercises: 46

Chapter 6: Living with Purpose 48

Chapter Summary: 48
    Key Lessons: 48
    Action Prompts (Reflective Questions): 50
    Life Changing Exercises: 55

Chapter 7: Strengthening Relationships 57

Chapter Summary: 57
    Key Lessons: 57
    Action Prompts (Reflective Questions): 59
    Life Changing Exercises: 64

Chapter 8: Living Mindfully 65

Chapter Summary: 65
    Key Lessons: 65
    Action Prompts (Reflective Questions): 67
    Life Changing Exercises: 72

Chapter 9: Preparing Spiritually..74
    Chapter Summary: 74
        Key Lessons:..74
        Action Prompts (Reflective Questions):........................76
        Life Changing Exercises: 81
Chapter 10: Practicing Gratitude 83
    Chapter Summary: 83
        Key Lessons:..83
        Action Prompts (Reflective Questions):........................85
        Life Changing Exercises: 90
Chapter 11: Sharing Hope 92
    Chapter Summary: 92
        Key Lessons:..92
        Action Prompts (Reflective Questions):........................93
        Life Changing Exercises: 98
Chapter 12: Cultivating Patience 100
    Chapter Summary: 100
        Key Lessons:..100
        Action Prompts (Reflective Questions):......................102
        Life Changing Exercises: 107
Chapter 13: Nurturing Compassion...............................109
    Chapter Summary: 109
        Key Lessons:..109
        Action Prompts (Reflective Questions):......................110

Life Changing Exercises: 114

Chapter 14: Persevering in Faith.. 116

    Chapter Summary: 116

        Key Lessons: 116

        Action Prompts (Reflective Questions): 118

        Life Changing Exercises: 122

Chapter 15: Celebrating Hope 124

    Chapter Summary: 124

        Key Lessons: 124

        Action Prompts (Reflective Questions): 125

        Life Changing Exercises: 130

Thank You 132

Free Audio Book 133

How To Use This Book?

Welcome to the "The Great Disappearance: 31 Ways to be Rapture Ready" workbook, which is intended to deepen your comprehension of Dr. David Jeremiah's game-changing discoveries. This workbook is designed to aid in your comprehension of the material by promoting contemplation, introspection, and the practical application of the ideas covered in the main book.

- Chapter Summary: Read the summary before starting each chapter. You will have a thorough knowledge of the key ideas covered by Dr. Jeremiah in "The Great Disappearance" after reading this succinct summary. It serves as a compass, directing you through the chapter's key lessons.
- Key Lessons: Discover the five main lessons that may be drawn from the main book. These lessons provide you with a solid understanding of the chapter's main ideas by distilling its fundamental ideas and insights. Consider how these teachings relate to your own views and experiences as you reflect on them.

- Action Prompts (Reflective Questions): Participate in the reflection exercises offered in each chapter. These questions are meant to inspire in-depth reflection and self-discovery. Consider these inquiries carefully, enabling your answers to disclose fresh perceptions of your faith, convictions, and spiritual path.
- Life Changing Exercises: Engage in the transformative activities described in each chapter. These useful exercises are designed to motivate significant change in your life. These exercises, which range from journaling to artistic expression, provide you the power to put the main book's lessons into practice while promoting your own personal and spiritual development.
- Community Engagement: Think about starting or joining a discussion group with other "The Great Disappearance" readers. You can improve your comprehension and strengthen your relationship to the subject matter by participating in discussions, exchanging reflections, and offering support to one another.

- Celebrate Your Progress: As you complete the workbook, acknowledge your development and progress. Recognize the beneficial adjustments you've made to your outlook, habits, and faith. Each step taken toward spiritual maturity is a noteworthy accomplishment worth celebrating.
- Keep Your Mind and Heart Open: Enter each chapter with an open mind and an open heart. Allow Dr. Jeremiah's lessons to upend your assumptions, deepen your comprehension, and motivate your spiritual development. Accept the chance for development and change.

Your travels toward spiritual readiness are profound and instructive, and this workbook is your companion. I pray that reading "The Great Disappearance: 31 Ways to be Rapture Ready" will lead to new understandings, self-discoveries, and a stronger bond with your religion. Happy learning and many blessings on your transformational journey.

Overview Of The Book

The idea of the Rapture, as explained in "The Great Disappearance: 31 Ways to be Rapture Ready" by Dr. David Jeremiah, emerges as a beacon of hope and spiritual readiness in the constantly shifting landscape of our world, where political unrest, economic uncertainty, and social divisions seem to dominate the narrative. The in-depth examination of biblical prophecy concerning the Rapture by Dr. Jeremiah provides believers seeking comfort in difficult times with more than simply a look into the future. This transformative book left me feeling incredibly touched, motivated and challenged as I read through its pages. I felt the need to create a guided diary workbook to help readers on their spiritual path since I was so concerned about being Rapture-ready.

Book Summary:

Dr. David Jeremiah's book "The Great Disappearance: 31 Ways to be Rapture Ready" goes deeply into the core of biblical prophecy, revealing the secrets surrounding the Rapture, a crucial aspect of Christian eschatology. Dr. Jeremiah's words ring urgently in the face of global uncertainties, reminding readers that blessed are those who hunger for the return of their Saviour in the midst of upheaval. The key issues covered in the book are who will be raptured, when it will happen, and what will happen to those who miss it. Dr. Jeremiah dismantles sensationalism by conducting a thorough analysis of significant biblical texts and historical context, giving readers a firm foundation based on God's Word.

I felt a strong need to share this life-changing event with others after being greatly moved by the message of hope and readiness presented in "The Great Disappearance." As a result, the concept for a prompted/guided journal workbook emerged. The goal of the companion workbook is to encourage readers to connect with Dr. Jeremiah's teachings more deeply by giving them a structured setting in which to consider, internalise, and put the profound insight from the main book into practice.

Motives behind the Workbook's creation:

- Encouraging Deeper Reflection: The Rapture is a deeply personal and intimate journey of faith, not merely a theological idea. The workbook asks users to consider their opinions, concerns, and expectations in relation to this occurrence, encouraging a profound spiritual introspection.

- Encouraging Practical Application: Dr. Jeremiah's book offers a wealth of insights, but it can be difficult to translate those insights into practical actions. The workbook provides useful tasks to help readers apply the lessons to their everyday lives and develop a sincere Rapture-ready attitude.
- Creating Community: Sharing spiritual adventures can have a greater influence. The workbook includes group exercises, topics for discussion, and questions for reflection, fostering a sense of community among readers. Sharing ideas and experiences helps increase comprehension and faith.
- Increasing Scripture Engagement: The workbook invites readers to explore pertinent biblical passages and provides a series of questions to help with understanding. The teachings of Dr. Jeremiah are more powerful when they are applied directly to Scripture, which strengthens the theme of readiness.

- Fostering Personal Transformation: The workbook seeks to transform the heart in addition to the mind. Readers are challenged to face their concerns, doubts, and uncertainties through self-evaluation tools and guided prayers, which eventually results in a strengthened faith in God's purpose.

This workbook was essentially created as a labour of love and trust to further the profound message of hope and readiness found in "The Great Disappearance." It is my honest hope that readers of this workbook will embrace the Rapture as a liberating, life-changing truth in addition to understanding its significance. May it act as a beacon, leading readers towards spiritual preparation and bringing them closer to the joyous expectation of Christ's second coming.

Chapter 1: Embracing the Imminence

Chapter Summary:

This chapter explores the idea of iminence and emphasises the urgency and imminence of the Rapture as it is described in the main book. It challenges readers to consider how they perceive this event, evaluate how it affects their day-to-day lives, and take proactive measures to set their priorities in line with the expectation of Christ's second coming.

Key Lessons:

- The Rapture is a near-term occurrence, highlighting the importance of maintaining ongoing alertness and readiness in our spiritual journey.
- Our daily priorities should be revised to place more emphasis on spiritual development and living with a kingdom perspective in light of the approaching return of Christ.

- Believing in the imminent Rapture gives people a sense of urgency about spreading the good news of salvation to others.
- As we wait for Christ's coming, setting personal goals that are centred on spiritual preparedness will make life more meaningful and rewarding.
- In spite of the difficulties and uncertainties of life, anticipating the Rapture helps people feel hopeful and joyful.

Action Prompts (Reflective Questions):

After reading about the imminent Rapture in the main book, how has your understanding of it changed?

_____
_____
_____
_____

Consider your priorities and day-to-day activities. How can the idea of imminence affect your decisions and behaviour?

What concrete objectives can you establish for yourself to better connect your life with the expectation of Christ's second coming?

Take into account the individuals in your life who might not be aware of the Rapture or its significance. How are you going to deliver this message to them?

_____

_____

_____

_____

_____

_____

_____

_____

_____

_____

_____

How may your attitude towards problems and issues in your daily life be impacted by the sense of urgency brought on by the Rapture?

_____
_____
_____
_____
_____
_____
_____
_____
_____
_____
_____

Life Changing Exercises:

- Write down your thoughts and reflections on the idea of imminence and its consequences for your life in a journal every day for a week.
- Make a vision board or other visual representation of your own objectives for rapture preparedness and spiritual development.
- Name someone in your life who would gain from knowing more about the Rapture. Start a discussion with them on this subject.
- Create a "spiritual priority" checklist to keep you focused on what's most important in light of Christ's impending return.
- Participate in a community service or outreach project as a method to actively spread the good news of the impending Rapture.

Chapter 2: Understanding the Signs

Chapter Summary:

Readers of Dr. David Jeremiah's book "The Great Disappearance: 31 Ways to be Rapture Ready" are led through an examination of the signs of the times as outlined in the main book. In today's society, Dr. Jeremiah stresses the need to comprehend and identify these indications. Biblical prophecies are examined in light of current international events to offer light on their importance in the context of the end times. The chapter exhorts readers to be watchful and spiritually ready by asking them to ponder on the indicators and how they affect their faith and behaviour.

Key Lessons:

- The chapter emphasises the importance of recognising and comprehending the signs of the times, highlighting their applicability in the context of biblical prophecy.

- Biblical Relevance: Readers get insight into how biblical prophesies relate to modern world events, demonstrating the timeless relevance of Scripture.
- Faith in the Face of Uncertainty: The major lesson emphasises preserving and enhancing one's faith despite troubling indications and displaying confidence in God's plan.
- Practical Observation: The chapter promotes a proactive attitude towards spiritual preparation by encouraging readers to actively observe and journal about certain indicators they discern.
- The Importance of Preparedness: Readers are aware of the need to turn their comprehension of the signs into concrete steps, thereby emphasising the necessity of being ready for the Rapture.

Action Prompts (Reflective Questions):

Sign Awareness: What contemporary signs have you seen in your environment? How do these omens match up with the prophecies in the Bible?

Effect on Faith: Consider how your faith has been impacted by your awareness of these indications. Has it strengthened your faith in God's promises, or has it left you with doubts and questions?

_____

_____

_____

_____

_____

_____

_____

_____

_____

_____

_____

_____

Personal Response: In light of the signals you've seen, how do you feel compelled to respond? Are there any particular steps or mentality adjustments you feel God is pressing you to make?

_____

_____

_____

_____

_____

_____

_____

_____

_____

_____

_____

Sharing Insights: Think about sharing your findings with others. What kind of impact may sharing knowledge about the signs of the times have on your neighbourhood and fellow believers?

_____

_____

_____

_____

_____

_____

_____

_____

_____

_____

Reflective prayer: Spend some time in prayer asking God to help you interpret and react to the indications. How can prayer strengthen your faith and confidence as you face uncertain times?

_____

_____

_____

_____

_____

_____

_____

_____

_____

_____

_____

Life Changing Exercises:

- Sign diary: Start a diary that is solely intended for noting the indicators you notice in your daily life. Update it frequently with fresh insights and views.
- Bible Study: Explore biblical prophecies concerning current events. Spend time studying pertinent texts and learning more about their relevance.
- Prayer Vigil: Schedule routine times for prayer and thought on the indicators you've seen. In order to navigate these moments with faith, make use of this time to ask God for insight and direction.
- Community Discussion: Start a conversation on the signs of the times in your church or with a group of other believers. Discuss your thoughts, worries, and preparation techniques on a spiritual level.
- Action Plan: Create a workable action plan for spiritual readiness based on your reflections and insights. Include specific actions in the context of these indicators to bring your life into line with your religion.

Chapter 3: The Joy of Expectation

Chapter Summary:

Dr. David Jeremiah dives further into the wonderful delight that comes from looking forward to Christ's return, which is a major theme of "The Great Disappearance: 31 Ways to be Rapture Ready." He emphasises how important it is to live with hope and expectation, stressing that this happy anticipation should pervade every area of our life. We are inspired to adopt an optimistic view and a fresh perspective on the future as we investigate the joyful anticipation of Christ's return.

Key Lessons:

- Joy in Anticipation: Looking forward to Christ's second coming offers a special and profound joy that transcends everyday life.

- Inspiration through Hope: Consider times in your life when excitement provided you joy and inspiration, and use this inspiration to push on in your spiritual journey.
- A New Perspective: Develop a daily habit of happy anticipation and shift your perspective to one of optimism and hope.
- everlasting Perspective: Reorient your attention away from momentary issues and towards the everlasting hope of Christ's second coming, letting it guide your choices and priorities.
- Spreading the excitement: Be aware of the transformational potential of encouraging others to embrace hope by sharing the excitement of anticipation with them.

Action Prompts (Reflective Questions):

Anticipating Joy: How has the idea of anticipating Christ's return with joy changed the way you think about hope and joy?

_____

_____

_____

_____

_____

_____

_____

_____

_____

_____

_____

Personal Reflection: Think back on specific occasions in your life when anticipation inspired and gave joy. How can you use this inspiration to advance in your spiritual life?

_____
_____
_____
_____
_____
_____
_____
_____
_____
_____
_____

Daily Practise: How can you create a daily habit of happy anticipation, and how may this have a good effect on your view on life and mindset?

_____
_____
_____
_____
_____
_____
_____
_____
_____
_____
_____

Priorities: How can you change your focus from earthly issues to a more eternal viewpoint, guiding your choices in the expectation of Christ's second coming?

_____

_____

_____

_____

_____

_____

_____

_____

_____

_____

Spreading Hope: Think about the people in your life who could gain from the joyful anticipation of Christ's second coming. How can you impart this hope to them and encourage them to share it?

_____
_____
_____
_____
_____
_____
_____
_____
_____
_____
_____
_____

Life Changing Exercises:

- Joyful Anticipation Notebook: Begin a notebook where you can record times in your life when you feel joyful anticipation. Think about how this apprehension affects your disposition and drive.
- Create a set of daily affirmations that are centred on the joyful anticipation of Christ's return. Each morning, say these affirmations aloud to cultivate a happy outlook.
- Perform a prioritisation exercise to assess your current priorities and make necessary changes to bring them into line with an everlasting viewpoint. Think about how these adjustments might make your life more fulfilling and joyful.
- Identify at least one person in your life who could gain from learning about the joyful expectation of Christ's return. Sharing Hope Initiative. Reach out to them and start a dialogue about faith and hope.
- Community of Expectancy: Find or start a group of like-minded people who look forward to Christ's return. By banding together in this hope, you can

support one another and enhance your positive attitude on life.

Chapter 4: Strengthening Faith Amidst Chaos

Chapter Summary:

In this chapter, we examine the idea of fortifying our faith in the face of challenging situations. Dr. Jeremiah emphasizes the great ability of religion to uphold us during times of upheaval and uncertainty by using biblical references and personal experiences. This chapter serves as a reminder that religion is a dynamic force that can guide us through life's storms, not merely a passive belief.

Key Lessons:

- Faith as an Anchor: Faith offers stability and hope in the midst of upheaval, acting as an anchor during life's storms.
- Biblical Resilience: Investigating biblical characters who maintained their faith in the face of adversity might provide us with important insights into our own travels.

- Personal Faith Stories: Thinking back on instances in our lives where faith was essential will help us to have more faith in God's providence.
- Faith-Building practice: To strengthen our spiritual basis, it is crucial to establish a regular faith-building practice that includes prayer, Bible reading, and meditation.
- The importance of community: During stressful times, connecting with a faith group can offer crucial support and inspiration.

Action Prompts (Reflective Questions):

Which biblical character's faith narrative most closely resembles your present situation, and why?

_____

_____

_____

_____

_____
_____
_____
_____
_____
_____
_____

Personal Faith Milestones: Describe a time when your faith helped you get through a trying circumstance. What did you learn from the experience?

_____
_____
_____
_____
_____
_____
_____
_____

What does your current faith-building habit entail, and how might you improve it to be more resilient to chaos?

Take time to think about the impact that prayer has had on your life. How has prayer helped you to maintain your faith when things are difficult?

How can you connect with your religious community in order to find support and inspiration in the midst of chaos?

_____
_____
_____
_____
_____
_____
_____
_____
_____
_____
_____

Life Changing Exercises:

- Start a faith journal to record your moments of faith and confidence in God during trying times. Regularly review it for motivation.
- Daily Scripture Meditation: Set aside some time each day to reflect on verses from the Bible that encourage perseverance and faith. Keep a thought and insight journal.
- Plan a brief retreat that focuses on prayer and introspection. Use this opportunity to strengthen your faith and ask God for direction.
- Participate in a faith-based community activity or initiative to strengthen the bonds of support and community among Christians.
- Faith Mentorship: Look for a mentor or spiritual leader who can help you through the chaos of life by providing guidance and inspiration. Study their knowledge and experiences.

Chapter 5: Facing Fears and Doubts

Chapter Summary:

In this crucial section of "The Great Disappearance," Dr. David Jeremiah discusses the normal human anxieties and uncertainties that arise while thinking about the Rapture. He offers an understanding of the worries that may surface when Christians struggle with the ambiguities of this occurrence. As a step towards spiritual preparation, Dr. Jeremiah emphasises the significance of admitting and facing these anxieties and scepticism.

Key Lessons:

- Understanding the Source: Uncertainty and false information are frequently to blame for worries and scepticism over the Rapture. It's critical to determine whether these emotions are a result of true worries or misunderstandings.

- The Importance of Community: Reaching out to other believers and looking for support within a community of faith can be a potent remedy for worries and scepticism. Anxieties can be lessened by exchanging knowledge and perspectives.
- Dr. Jeremiah emphasises the importance of prayer in overcoming worries and scepticism in his essay, "The Power of Prayer." In addition to fostering a closer relationship with God, prayer offers a forum for voicing worries and asking for spiritual direction.
- Biblical Assurance: Looking further into the Scriptures and developing a better understanding of the biblical basis for the Rapture can allay concerns and give comfort.
- Taking proactive measures to get ready for the Rapture can strengthen confidence and allay concerns. This is known as an action-oriented religion. A stronger, more certain belief can be attained by partaking in spiritual activities and looking for clarification on issues.

Action Prompts (Reflective Questions):

What specific apprehensions or scepticisms do you have about the Rapture? Give them some thought before recording them.

_____

_____

_____
_____
_____
_____

_____

_____

_____

_____

_____

Root exploration: Consider where these apprehensions and scepticisms came from. Did they draw inspiration from other sources or from your own life?

Community Connection: How has belonging to a faith-based community influenced your capacity to confront and get rid of these worries? Tell us about your experiences.

_____
_____
_____
_____
_____
_____
_____
_____
_____
_____
_____

How has prayer served as a tool for your spiritual path in terms of comfort and assurance? Do you have any specific worries or scepticisms you'd like to pray through with God?

_____

_____

_____

_____

_____

_____

_____

_____

_____

_____

Which verses or teachings from the Bible have brought you understanding and calm regarding the Rapture? How can you read the Bible more carefully to clear up your doubts?

Life Changing Exercises:

- Create a "fear journal" in which you can record your worries and scepticism regarding the Rapture over a predetermined amount of time. Keep track of any adjustments to your views and emotions.
- Community Engagement: Start discussions about worries and scepticism about the Rapture within your religious group. In order to create a friendly environment, share your experiences and pay attention to others.
- Praying: Set aside time each day to prayerfully discuss your concerns about the Rapture. Create a personal prayer plan to address and allay these worries.
- Engage in a careful study of biblical verses that address the Rapture. Think about signing up for a study group or asking an experienced mentor for advice.
- Create a workable action plan to actively get ready for the Rapture. This could be reading pertinent books, going to conferences, or conversing with other

believers. Observe your development and any changes in your faith and confidence.

Chapter 6: Living with Purpose

Chapter Summary:

Readers are pushed to explore their passions and talents in The Great Disappearance: 31 methods to be rapture ready, which helps them connect with God's divine purpose. In "Living with Purpose," Dr. David Jeremiah digs into the fundamental concept of purposeful living as presented in "The Great Disappearance: 31 Ways to be Rapture Ready." Dr. Jeremiah urges readers to think about how their actions might have a beneficial impact on others by highlighting the transformational power of living a purpose-driven life. This emphasises the need of being spiritually prepared in light of the impending Rapture.

Key Lessons:

- Divine Alignment: Finding purpose entails matching your interests and skills with God's bigger picture, making sure that your deeds reflect His intent.

- Impactful Living: Purposeful living has benefits that extend beyond personal fulfilment and have an impact on those in your immediate vicinity.
- Eternal importance: Living with purpose goes beyond the fleeting and ties your deeds to eternal importance, especially when it comes to spiritual readiness.
- Understanding your purpose entails sharing your talents with others, encouraging them, and pointing them in the direction of their own mission.
- Continuous Growth: Purpose-driven living is an ongoing process of self-discovery and growth that develops as your relationship with God and His teachings becomes more intimate.

Action Prompts (Reflective Questions):

How does connecting your interests and skills to God's plan make you feel content and closer to Him?

_____
_____
_____
_____
_____
_____
_____
_____
_____
_____
_____

How might your special abilities benefit your neighbourhood and the people there, enhancing their spiritual readiness?

Think back to times when you had a strong feeling of purpose. How did what you were doing fit into God's purpose for your life?

_____
_____
_____
_____
_____
_____
_____
_____
_____
_____

Think about the obligations that come with life with a purpose. How can you use your abilities to help others find their spiritual calling?

___
___
___
___
___
___
___
___
___
___
___

Consider your actions and activities right now. Do they support your goals? If not, what changes can you make to live a life that is more purpose-driven?

_____

_____

_____

_____

_____

_____

_____

_____

_____

_____

_____

Life Changing Exercises:

- Writing About Your Purpose: Schedule time each day to write in a journal about your goals. Think about your interests, skills, and the influence you hope to have. Reread and edit these entries frequently to keep on track with God's purpose for you.
- Take part in the "Acts of Kindness Challenge," during which you consciously carry out one act of kindness each day for a week. While understanding the effects of your intentional activities on others, record the responses and feelings of those you assist.
- Identify a member of your community who could profit from your knowledge or experiences by mentoring or sharing it. Encourage them to find their own purpose by offering to mentor them. This act of imparting knowledge can have a significant impact on both you and the mentoree.
- Attending a religious or community function with the goal of learning about others' goals is known as purposeful networking. Talk to people from different backgrounds to learn about their interests and how they fit with God's purpose. Your perspective will be

widened and your feeling of purpose will be strengthened by this practice.

- Retreat for prayer and meditation: Set aside a day for prayer and meditation to seek God's direction on your mission. Deeply examine yourself and ask God to reveal His purposes for your life. If you have any revelations or insights during this spiritual retreat, write them down so you may build your life around them.

Chapter 7: Strengthening Relationships

Chapter Summary:

In his book, Dr. David Jeremiah explores the enormous effects that the Rapture may have on our interpersonal bonds. In preparing for Christ's return, Jesus emphasises the value of love, forgiveness, and reconciliation. This chapter is a sobering reminder that, in light of the impending Rapture, promoting harmony and understanding in our relationships is not just a moral requirement but also a spiritual necessity.

Key Lessons:

- The Rapture emphasises the importance of love in our relationships. Love has an enduring power. Love takes on a leading role, transcending material worries and opening up opportunities for closer relationships.
- The Healing Power of Forgiveness: Forgiveness is a crucial component of being prepared for the Rapture. Not only does forgiving others heal relationships, but

it also gets our hearts ready for Christ's second coming.

- The spiritual practice of reconciliation reflects God's grace. By actively seeking to mend broken relationships, we are in harmony with divine principles and advance peace and harmony.
- The Rapture shows us the value of unity in the face of diversity. We might be more ready for the heavenly unity that will exist when Christ returns by accepting diversity and encouraging understanding among family members.
- Building Relationships Isn't Just an Academic Exercise: Building relationships isn't just an academic endeavour. It has to do with changing hearts. Our relationships develop into havens of acceptance and love as we mentally and spiritually prepare.

Action Prompts (Reflective Questions):

What impact has the idea of the Rapture had on the way you view love in relationships?

_____
_____
_____
_____
_____
_____
_____
_____
_____
_____
_____

Think back to a previous argument. What actions can you take to encourage reconciliation and restoration in that relationship?

_____

_____

_____

_____

_____

_____

_____

_____

_____

_____

Do you have any relationships in your life that require repair? What can you do right now to start the healing process?

How can you encourage unity while accepting differences by embracing the diversity in your relationships?

_____
_____
_____
_____
_____
_____
_____
_____
_____
_____

Think of a tense partnership. What particular steps can you take, regardless of how the other person responds, to get your heart ready for reconciliation?

Life Changing Exercises:

- Love in Action: Express your gratitude and admiration in sincere letters to the individuals you care about. This activity promotes affection and fortifies your ties.
- Starting a forgiveness notebook is a good idea. Keep a record of the times you have forgiven someone and the effects it had on your well-being. Use this as a reminder of the strength of forgiveness.
- Reconciliation Conversation: Start a dialogue with a person you've disagreed with. Approach the situation with humility, a sincere desire for a solution, and an awareness of others' perspectives.
- Engage with people who have diverse perspectives or ideologies. Participate in conversations or cultural events. Make use of the diversity all around you to promote harmony and understanding.
- Practise a heart-cleansing meditation with a focus on peace and forgiveness. In anticipation of the Rapture, use this meditation to purify your heart and get ready for fulfilling relationships.

Chapter 8: Living Mindfully

Chapter Summary:

Dr. David Jeremiah emphasizes the transforming potential of mindfulness as a spiritual practice in his book. The exploration of mindfulness encourages readers to strengthen their relationship with God. In this chapter, we'll look at how being in the moment can improve spiritual awareness and promote a deep sense of serenity and understanding in one's spiritual path.

Key Lessons:

- A direct relationship with God and His presence in ordinary situations is made possible by the spiritual practice of mindfulness, which is not merely a secular practice.
- Developing Presence: Being fully present in every moment enables one to have a more meaningful

spiritual experience by being more conscious of God's grace, love, and direction.
- Creating a sacred space where people can hear God's voice and more clearly discern His intentions, mindfulness practices help quiet the cacophony of the outside world.
- Gratitude and mindfulness: Gratitude creates mindfulness, which helps people recognize the beauty of God's creations and grow more reverent of His divine plan.
- Christians who practice mindfulness can develop a compassionate heart that reflects God's goodness and love in their dealings with others.

Action Prompts (Reflective Questions):

Consider the Presence: How frequently do you experience being totally in the present and experiencing the divine presence all around you? What breaks up your attentiveness in everyday life?

_____

_____

_____

_____

_____

_____

_____

_____

_____

_____

Moments of Spiritual Connection: Think back to times when practicing mindfulness strengthened your relationship with God. What behaviors or settings help you feel this connection?

_____

_____

_____

_____

_____

_____

_____

_____

_____

_____

_____

Silencing the Noise: What internal or external factors make it difficult for you to hear God clearly? How can you make a peaceful environment for prayerful communication with God?

Reflect on the part that gratitude has played in your spiritual development. How does mindfulness improve your capacity to express gratitude for the many and tiny benefits in your life?

Consider instances where practicing mindfulness improved your interactions with others. This is compassion in action. How can you show mindful compassion to those who test your tolerance or comprehension?

Life Changing Exercises:

- Daily Mindful Moments: Set aside at least 10 minutes each day for quiet thought and mindful breathing. Appreciate God's presence in your surroundings and only think on the now.
- Take a thoughtful stroll around the outdoors while paying special attention to the sights, sounds, and smells that surround you. Consider the exquisite beauty of nature and God's handiwork.
- Start a thankfulness diary and list three things each day for which you are grateful. While writing, practice mindfulness and completely experience the feelings of thankfulness.
- Practice a loving-kindness meditation by thinking lovingly and compassionately of yourself, your loved ones, your acquaintances, and even your enemies. Develop empathy and a sense of connection.
- Mindful Eating: Make an effort to eat mindfully each day. Take your time, enjoy every meal, and be thankful

for the food. Consider the relationship between your physical and spiritual well-being.

Chapter 9: Preparing Spiritually

Chapter Summary:

Dr. David Jeremiah examines the crucial subject of spiritual readiness for the impending Rapture in his book. By concentrating on the fundamental elements of spiritual development, he helps readers see the need to strengthen their relationship with God. In order to be prepared for the Rapture, the chapter places a strong emphasis on the necessity for introspection and the creation of a unique spiritual growth plan that includes prayer, study, and service.

Key Lessons:

- Take a spiritual inventory to determine your strengths and places for development. This is important for assessing your spiritual development.
- Consistent Growth: Recognise that spiritual development is a continual process that calls for

consistent effort, devotion, and a readiness to progress.

- A Connection Through Prayer: Use the transformative power of prayer to deepen your relationship with God and ask for His direction in all areas of your life.
- Knowledge through Study: Recognise the importance of carefully studying the Scriptures to achieve significant insights that foster spiritual maturity and provide you with the tools you need to meet obstacles with faith.
- Service and Compassion: Recognise the positive social effects of selfless service and compassion, demonstrating God's love through deeds of kindness and assisting others in their spiritual preparation.

Action Prompts (Reflective Questions):

Self-Reflection: Which facets of your spiritual life give you the greatest joy and where do you think there is room for development?

_____

_____

_____

_____

_____

_____

_____

_____

_____

_____

_____

Commitment to Growth: How can you designate time specifically for prayer, meditation, and Bible study in order to consistently pursue spiritual growth?

___

___

___

___

___

___

___

___

___

___

Prayerful Objectives: What particular areas of your life do you need God's direction in? Create goals that are based on prayer, asking for heavenly help in these areas.

_____

_____

_____

_____

_____

_____

_____

_____

_____

_____

_____

Developing Knowledge: What parts of the Bible most interest you? Make a study plan to go further into these subjects and strengthen your faith.

_____

_____

_____

_____

_____

_____

_____

_____

_____

_____

_____

_____

Service to Others: How can you give back to your church or community? Find opportunities where your interests and skills match those of others, encouraging a spirit of service and compassion.

Life Changing Exercises:

- Daily Devotion: Create a daily devotional schedule, designating a certain period of time each day for prayer, meditation, and Scripture reading. Joy down your thoughts and prayers in a journal.
- Scripture Memorization: Select essential Bible verses that have to do with spiritual readiness and commit them to memory. Consider their implications and how they might influence your behaviour.
- Volunteer Service: Work as a volunteer in your church or community. Spend a few hours per week promoting kindness and love for a cause that speaks to your ideals.
- Seek a spiritual mentor or sign up for a Bible study group. To increase your understanding of faith, participate in conversations, pose inquiries to seasoned believers, and pick their brains.
- Random Acts of Kindness: Every day, carry out one act of random kindness. It might be anything as straightforward as a smile, a praise, or lending a helping hand. Consider how these deeds support your

spiritual development as you work to develop a compassionate and generous heart.

Chapter 10: Practicing Gratitude

Chapter Summary:

Dr. David Jeremiah examines the transforming potential of thankfulness in the context of spiritual preparedness in his book, "Practising Gratitude." This chapter emphasizes the crucial role that gratitude plays in helping us to align our hearts with God's purpose, cultivate a positive outlook, and strengthen our relationship with God. By practicing gratitude, we spiritually readied ourselves for the impending Rapture, finding courage and joy even in trying circumstances.

Key Lessons:

- Gratitude as a Spiritual Anchor: Gratitude acts as a fundamental component in enhancing our spiritual toughness by acting as a steady anchor in the presence of uncertainty.

- Perspective Shift: Embracing thankfulness causes us to see the plethora of benefits all around us rather than only what we lack, which promotes satisfaction and calm.
- Improving Spiritual Readiness: A grateful heart is more responsive to God's instructions and direction, which improves our readiness for the Rapture.
- Expressing thankfulness as a form of worship: Expressing gratitude not only strengthens our relationship with the divine, it also acts as a form of devotion.
- Gratitude in Adversity: Developing an attitude of gratitude in all situations, including difficult ones, builds our faith and fortitude and equips us for the uncertainties of the future.

Action Prompts (Reflective Questions):

Consider Your Blessings: Name three blessings in your life for which you are sincerely grateful.

_____

_____

_____

_____

_____

_____

_____

_____

_____

_____

Gratitude notebook: Begin a gratitude notebook and consider how these blessings have influenced your spiritual development. Every day, list at least one thing for which you are grateful. How does this routine affect your attitude toward life in general?

Finding Gratitude in Difficulties: Consider a recent difficulty you encountered. Consider any advantages or things you could have learnt from the event. How can thankfulness discovered even under difficult circumstances?

_____
_____
_____
_____
_____
_____
_____
_____
_____
_____
_____
_____

Showing Appreciation: Get in touch with someone who has made a difference in your life. Thank them and tell them how their influence has influenced your spiritual development. How does showing thankfulness improve your interpersonal connections?

_____
_____
_____
_____
_____
_____
_____
_____
_____
_____
_____

Gratitude in Prayer: During your time of prayer, concentrate only on thanking God. How can this concentrated act of gratitude strengthen your relationship with God?

Life Changing Exercises:

- Create a gratitude jar and ask family members or close friends to frequently add notes of thanks. Together, read these messages from time to time to cultivate a spirit of thankfulness.
- Gratitude Walk: Go on a walk of gratitude in the wilderness. Consider the beauty around you while you stroll and give thanks for creation's finer nuances. How does this routine help you appreciate God's creation more?
- Random Acts of Gratitude: Throughout the course of the week, perform random deeds of gratitude and goodwill. This can be sending a thank-you card, complimenting someone, or just showing gratitude to total strangers. How does sharing your thankfulness affect the way you connect with others?
- thankfulness Visualization: Perform a visualization exercise of thankfulness while you are meditating or praying. Imagine several facets of your existence and give thanks for each one. How can this visualization improve your level of spiritual readiness and contentment?

- Establish a regular thankfulness practice where you give thanks for specific blessings from the day, either before meals or before going to bed. How does this practice help you feel finished and at peace at the end of the day?

Chapter 11: Sharing Hope

Chapter Summary:

The transformational effect of sharing hope with others is the main topic of this chapter. In light of the Rapture, Dr. David Jeremiah emphasizes the importance of sharing the message of hope and faith. The chapter examines real-world examples of how hope has profoundly impacted people, highlighting the crucial role that believers play in illuminating the way for others in adversity.

Key Lessons:

- Sharing hope has a contagious impact. This is because it not only makes people feel better but also encourages others.
- Personal Stories Inspire: Personal stories of hope from real people inspire and reverberate strongly, strengthening faith in God's promises.
- Faith in Action: Actively communicating one's faith is a privilege as well as a duty since it enables believers to take part in God's plan of salvation for mankind.

- Compassion Bridges Gaps: Expressing hope via compassion helps to close gaps between people and promotes empathy, unity, and understanding.
- Eternal Impact: Sharing hope has eternal value and may influence someone's fate. It is not limited to this life.

Action Prompts (Reflective Questions):

Consider the impact: Recall a time when someone gave you hope. What effect did it have on your perspective, and what did you take away from it?

_____
_____
_____
_____
_____
_____
_____

_____

_____

_____

_____

Determine Your Special Message: Take into account your own spiritual development. What features of your tale can inspire others? How do you successfully express it?

_____

_____

_____

_____

_____

_____

_____

_____

_____

_____

Overcoming Barriers: Consider any reservations or anxieties you may have about expressing your beliefs. What actions can you take to go through these obstacles and confidently spread hope?

_____

_____

_____

_____

_____

_____

_____

_____

_____

_____

_____

Show Empathy: Imagine yourself in someone else's position, especially if that person is going through a trying period. How would you like to be given inspiration and hope? How would you go about doing it similarly?

_____
_____
_____
_____
_____
_____
_____
_____
_____
_____

Commit to Consistent Actions: What consistent daily or weekly behaviors can you commit to that promote hope? Sending a supportive message or paying attention to someone who is in need could suffice.

_____

_____

_____

_____

_____

_____

_____

_____

_____

_____

_____

Life Changing Exercises:

- Start a journal of hope: Start a journal in which you record all instances of hope, both those you experience yourself and those you share with others. Regularly consider these entries.
- Engage in conversations with friends, family, or coworkers to practice active listening. Engage in active listening without passing judgement and look for chances to give their worries some optimism.
- Plan a Community Hope Event: Arrange a community gathering that is centered on faith and hope. It might be a workshop, seminar, or even a social gathering. Use this occasion as a forum to share motivational tales.
- Send Personalised Messages: Spend some time sending individualized messages of faith and hope to others in your network. You can convey your concern and faith through them through handwritten letters, emails, or even voice messages.
- Volunteer for Hope Initiatives: Join groups or projects that promote hope, whether it's through counselling, mentoring, or charitable work. By taking part in such

endeavours, you not only benefit others but also gain a deeper comprehension of the significance of hope.

Chapter 12: Cultivating Patience

Chapter Summary:

In this chapter, we explore the fundamental idea of developing patience while anticipating the soon coming of Christ. This chapter serves as a spiritual road map, highlighting the value of patience as a transformational virtue that enables believers to face obstacles head-on with unwavering confidence.

Key Lessons:

- Divine Timing: Recognise the precision of God's timing. Patience entails believing in God's purpose even when it seems chaotic outside.
- Patience in the Face of Challenges: Patience isn't just about waiting; it's also about facing challenges head-on with grace and fortitude, confident that God will bring good out of them.

- Patience is a spiritual practice that bolsters your faith. It promotes spiritual development and emphasizes reliance on God's knowledge.
- Increasing Empathy: Patience training improves empathy, allowing you to comprehend others' hardships and respond to them with kindness and understanding.
- Serenity in the Face of Uncertainty: Patience training offers a deep sense of serenity, enabling believers to face uncertainty with a peaceful faith in God's providence.

Action Prompts (Reflective Questions):

Consider Your Approach to Waiting: What is your usual approach to waiting? What feelings and ideas come to mind? How can you change your viewpoint such that you see waiting as a chance for development?

Identify Impatience Triggers: What conditions or scenarios are the most likely to make you impatient? How can you avoid these triggers in the future and react patiently?

_____

_____

_____

_____

_____

_____

_____

_____

_____

_____

_____

Relationship Patience: Take into account how you interact with others. Do you ever let impatience affect your relationships? What actions may you take to practice tolerance with others?

Believing in God's Timing: Think back to a time when you were impatient. Can you now see how God's timing was in play? How can you use this insight to address your present problems?

Accepting Delays: Consider a desire or objective you have. How can you tackle any unforeseen delays with faith and patience? What can you discover while you wait?

Life Changing Exercises:

- Keep a daily patience journal to record times when your patience was put to the test and how you handled it. Consider your feelings and the results. Watch for trends and growth regions throughout time.
- Receptivity Meditation: Engage in mindfulness techniques while concentrating on the present. Embrace the quiet and calm as you develop patience in your daily life by learning to appreciate each moment without rushing.
- Random Acts of Kindness: Consistently perform acts of kindness. In addition to having a beneficial impact on others, doing so teaches patience as you wait for the seeds of kindness to take root and change the lives of others.
- Study the Bible's passages and narratives that emphasize patience. Think over these verses, realizing the importance of patience in the lives of biblical characters. Utilize these lessons in your situation.
- Prayer and Surrender: As you pray, give God your worries and frustration. Ask God for the endurance

and fortitude to wait patiently for His perfect timing. Let God change your heart and turn your impatience into steadfast faith.

Chapter 13: Nurturing Compassion

Chapter Summary:

Dr. David Jeremiah explores the compassion of Christ in great detail in this chapter, highlighting the transformative impact of compassion in our lives. He demonstrates via many examples how deeds of compassion and empathy can effect significant change, showing the love of Christ for others.

Key Lessons:

- Compassion as Christ's Essence: Showing Christ's love and mercy in concrete ways, compassion is the very essence of Christ.
- Transformative Impact: Compassionate actions have the ability to change circumstances and provide those in need hope and healing.
- Exemplifying Christ's Love: By cultivating compassion, we can reflect Christ's love and make His presence known in the lives of others.

- Empathy Creates Connection: Compassion creates strong bonds between people, dismantling obstacles and promoting understanding.
- The Ripple Effect: One act of kindness can start a chain reaction that influences others to show kindness and improves communities.

Action Prompts (Reflective Questions):

Consider Moments of Compassion: Think back to times in your life when compassion truly made a difference. What impact did these experiences have on how you view empathy?

_____

_____

_____

_____

_____

_____

_____

Seek out opportunities for compassion in your regular contacts. Where can you, even in little ways, bring compassion into your interactions with others?

Overcoming Obstacles: What difficulties do you encounter when exhibiting compassion? How can you get through them? Think about any biases or judgments that prevent you from acting with empathy.

_____

_____

_____

_____

_____

_____

_____

_____

_____

_____

Creating Bridges: Think about a person with whom you might struggle to empathize. How can you develop empathy and compassion for them?

_____

_____

_____

_____

_____

_____

_____

_____

_____

_____

_____

Reflecting Christ's Compassion: How may you show someone in need that you care about them in real ways? Come up with a list of realistic steps you can take to make a difference.

_____
_____
_____
_____
_____
_____
_____
_____
_____
_____

Life Changing Exercises:

- Random Acts of Kindness: Make a commitment to carry out one act of kindness every day for a week. A simple smile, a thoughtful remark, or assisting someone in need could suffice.

- Volunteer Experience: Commit a few hours to work at a nearby nonprofit organization or community center. Directly interact with those in need to better comprehend their struggles and demonstrate compassion.
- Compassion Journal: Keep a journal of your compassionate deeds and how they affect others. Consider how these encounters have affected your religion and character.
- Empathy in Conflict: When there are disagreements or conflicts, communicate kindly. Even in trying circumstances, try to grasp the other person's point of view in order to create empathy.
- Kindness Accountability Join forces with a friend or relative to support one another in cultivating compassion. Share your successes, setbacks, and victories with one another to spur one another on in this changing path.

Chapter 14: Persevering in Faith

Chapter Summary:

Dr. David Jeremiah discusses the subject of persistence in the face of difficulties in his book," highlighting its critical function in spiritual development. This chapter emphasizes the transforming potential of persevering in faith in the face of difficulties, showing how hardships can act as stepping stones toward a closer relationship with God.

Key Lessons:

- Enduring Faith Molds Character: Through perseverance, believers can emulate Christ's unwavering faith in the face of hardship.
- Challenges Help Us Develop Spiritual Resilience: Trials help us develop spiritual resiliency by teaching us to trust God's time and plan.

- Perseverance Deepens Trust: Overcoming hardships strengthens our reliance on God's grace and provision by deepening our faith in His trustworthiness.
- Growth Through Adversity: Every challenge confronted with faith is a chance for spiritual development, resulting in a deeper comprehension of God's love and omnipotence.
- Perseverance Brings Hope: By clinging to our faith despite difficulties, we discover hope in the knowledge that God's promises are steadfast even in the midst of life's storms.

Action Prompts (Reflective Questions):

Consider Your Trials Think about a difficult circumstance in your life where you showed tenacity. How did your faith help you get through that period?

___
___
___
___
___
___
___
___
___
___

Identify Possibilities for Growth Consider a recent court case. What revelations about God's nature, your own fortitude, and faith in His purpose did you gain?

_____

_____

_____

_____

_____

_____

_____

_____

_____

_____

Assess Your Trust: Consider how much you currently rely on God in trying times. What areas do you find difficult to trust His direction in?

_____

_____

_____

_____

_____

_____

_____

_____

_____

_____

_____

Recall a former challenge that resulted in unanticipated blessings or chances. How did God make a difficult situation into a reason for hope?

_____

_____

_____

_____

_____

_____

_____

_____

_____

_____

_____

The Importance of Group: Think about how your support network of friends or your religious group encouraged you to persevere. How can you use these connections to your advantage in upcoming trials?

_____

_____

_____

_____

_____

_____

_____

_____

_____

_____

_____

Life Changing Exercises:

- Start a gratitude journal with the express purpose of jotting down instances of fortitude and God's faithfulness in the midst of hardships. To develop a resilient attitude, review it often.

- Daily Bible meditation: Pick a scripture or verses from the Bible that speak to endurance, such as Romans 5:3-5 or James 1:1Let these texts encourage and bolster your faith when you encounter difficulties.
- Prayer and Surrender: Set out some time each day to pray explicitly about your struggles, giving God your worries and fears. Trust Him to bring you serenity and direction.
- Share Your Story: Share your testimony of endurance in your church community or with a friend. Acknowledging God's faithfulness in public increases your own belief and encourages others.
- Kindness: Show kindness to others and assist them when they go through difficult times. By encouraging others to endure, you strengthen your own fortitude and confidence in God's plan despite challenges.

Chapter 15: Celebrating Hope

Chapter Summary:

In his book, Dr. David Jeremiah explores the powerful sense of hope that springs from the expectation of Christ's second coming. This chapter emphasizes the transforming potential of predicting a future rooted in faith, resonating with the essence of hope in the face of uncertainty.

Key Lessons:

- Faith as an Anchor of Hope Recognise hope as a fundamental pillar of your spiritual journey that provides resiliency and strength in the face of difficulties.
- Community and Shared Expectancy: Recognise the importance of community hope since sharing in the expectancy of Christ's return with other Christians makes it richer.

- Eternal Perspective: Adopt an eternal viewpoint, understanding that the hope in Christ's second coming transcends adversity in the here and now and offers enduring consolation.
- Living with Purpose: Recognise that while you wait for Christ to return, your hope motivates you to live with a purpose, having a positive impact on others.
- Joyful expectation: Develop a sense of joyous expectation by letting hope pervade your everyday activities and encouraging thankfulness and optimism.

Action Prompts (Reflective Questions):

Embracing Hope: How does the idea of looking forward to Christ's return affect how you approach difficulties in life? Think back to a time when hope got you through a challenging situation.

_____

_____

_____

_____

Community Connection: Think about how important it is to spread your hope. How can you support other Christians as they wait for Christ to come back? Think about the benefits of shared hope for religious communities.

_____

_____

_____

_____

_____

_____

_____

Eternal Perspective Check: Consider a difficult circumstance you are presently dealing with. How do your outlook and behavior alter when you see it from an everlasting perspective that is rooted in the expectation of Christ's second coming?

_____

_____

_____

_____

Living with Purpose: How is the expectation of Christ's return motivating you to live with intention and make a good difference in the lives of others? Consider specific steps you might take to live in accordance with this noble desire.

Fostering Joy: Consider times in your life when you felt joyous in anticipation of Christ's coming again. How can you consistently practice happy anticipation in your day-to-day activities?

_____

_____

_____

_____

_____

_____

_____

Life Changing Exercises:

- Hope Record: Begin a record of hope. Keep a running journal of the times that your hope in Christ's return affected your choices, feelings, or interactions. Think back on these entries for inspiration through trying times.
- Hope-Fueled Acts: Perform acts of charity and kindness that are motivated by your hope in Christ. Donate, volunteer, or support a cause while imbuing all of your deeds with the upbeat expectation of the Rapture.

- Host a community celebration with the subject of hope as its focal point. Invite speakers or plan events that emphasise the hope of Christ's second coming. To generate a sense of shared hope, encourage attendees to share their personal stories.
- Creative Expression: Use art to creatively express your hope. Create a work of art, a poem, or a song with the anticipation of Christ's coming as your inspiration. Use your imagination to remind yourself of the immense hope you possess.
- Hope-Filled Conversations: Have discussions with loved ones about the hope that comes from Christ's second coming. Talk about your experiences and hear others out. Take advantage of the chance to encourage one another's faith as you discuss the Rapture.

Thank You

Your Opinion Matters!

Our dedicated team of editors and writers poured their hearts into crafting this workbook to deliver the best for you. We even went the extra mile to provide a **FREE AUDIO VERSION** for your convenience.

Has this book made a positive impact on you? If so, we'd be thrilled to hear about it! **Scan the QR Code below to share your thoughts and leave a review.**

Free Audio Book

Scan the QR Code below to Download the Audio Book Version COMPLETELY FREE.

Thank you for being a part of our journey!

Made in United States
Orlando, FL
14 April 2024